I Am Supernatural
Walking in Spiritual Gifts

Book Four
Walking with Jesus
Becoming the Best Me I Can Be

Pamela D White

A publication of Blooming Desert Ministries

ISBN 978-1-7370802-6-8 (sc print)
ISBN 978-1-7370802-7-5 (ebook)

Printed in the United States of America
Copyright © 2021 by Pamela D White
All Rights Reserved.

IngramSparks Publishing (Ingram: Lightning Source, LLC)

One Ingram Blvd., La Vergne, TN 37086

Publishing Note: Publishing style capitalizes certain pronouns in Scriptures that refer to the Father, Son, and Holy Spirit, and may differ from other publishing styles. **All emphasis in the Scriptures' quotations is the authors.** The name satan and related names are not capitalized as the author's preference not to acknowledge him, even though it violates grammatical rules.

PDW PUBLICATIONS

Dedication

This book series is dedicated to you.

Everyone has opportunities to become a better version of themselves. My prayer is that this book series helps you on that journey. The Lord loves you so much He desires an intimate relationship with you. You are special to Him and He loves spending time with you. Walking and talking with Jesus every day should be the norm, not the exception. Life can bring difficult circumstances and situations. When you walk with Jesus, life events, are not only manageable but can be turned for your good.

"And we know that all things work together for good to those who love God, to those who are the called according to His purpose," Romans 8:28.

Come with me into this exploration of how you can develop a relationship with Jesus and walk with Him every day. This is an opportunity to become a better you.

Acknowledgments

The Great Commission given by our Lord and Savior Jesus Christ noted in Matthew 28:16-20 is my inspiration for this publication. Verses 19-20 state, *"Go therefore and make disciples of all the nations, baptizing them in the name of the Father and of the Son and of the Holy Spirit, teaching them to observe all things that I have commanded you; and lo, I am with you always, even to the end of the age."* This verse is the very basis for missionary work all over the globe. I have been blessed to be able to serve in a few of those missions. Missions are an amazing experience. I came to realize though that everyone cannot always do all the parts commanded in these verses. I can't always go. I didn't often get to baptize. What I realized was that I can do my part in teaching to observes the truths of the Scriptures. My desire to fulfill the teaching part of the Great Commission was the inspiration for this work. My pastor, Bishop Larry Taylor, and First Lady Desetra Taylor allowed our church to use these Bible studies in our New Life Discipleship classes for nearly twenty years. The work has also been used in prison ministries in central Illinois for as many years. The teaching has proven effective in changing many lives and discipling the children of God. Thank you, Bishop and First Lady, for teaching a balanced spiritual and natural life so I could complete this project and see the impact of the work on people's lives.

Bishop positioned me to be the director of New Life Ministries Discipleship for several years. New Life classes were designed to teach those new to Christianity or new to the church the foundational truths needed to build a solid life in Christ. During that time, this work was fine-tuned with the help and input from the dedicated, gifted, and anointed New Life teachers Minister Retta Smith, Minister James Smith, Minister Debby Henkel, Dr. Terry Husband, Minister Char-Michelle McDowell, Minister Yvonne Smith, Minister Herbert Smyer, and Professor Susan Gibson along with the encouragement and guidance of Dr. Chequita Brown and community service advocate Minister Patricia Turner. I also want to give a shout-out to Dr. Wanda Turner, nationally acclaimed minister, teacher, prophet, life coach, mentor, and best-selling author, who continued to encourage me to just publish the thing! Thanks to all of you. Each of you has made a significant impact on my life.

My dear friend and mentor, First Lady Marshell Wickware, supported the project and pushed me to publish it for years. Thanks for not giving up on me!

My life-long friend, Robin McClallen, thank you for all your support, input, and encouraging me to publish something. You have been instrumental in making me an author.

A special thanks to my husband, Brian K. White, for his patience and prayers as I spent hours and hours researching, writing, and rewriting. Thanks, BW!

Most of all thank you to the Holy Spirit and my Lord and Savior Jesus Christ. I present this work in obedience and honor to You.

Contents

Book Four

I Am Supernatural
Walking in Spiritual Gifts

OBJECTIVE

Book Two introduced the character and nature of the Holy Spirit. This lesson seeks to provide an understanding of how the Holy Spirit works through you to build the church and edify other believers. To accomplish this task, the Holy Spirit equips you with supernatural powers - Spiritual Gifts. We will summarize the gifts given by the Holy Spirit. It will assist you in understanding your specific gift set and how God desires for you to use the gifts He has given you.

MEMORY VERSE

"Now concerning spiritual gifts, brothers, I would not have you ignorant...Now there are diversities of gifts, but the same Spirit" 1 Corinthians 12:1, 4 AKJV.

I Am Supernatural

A. **Understanding Spiritual Gifts**
    1. Purpose of Spiritual Gifts
    2. Spiritual Gifts and Talent

B. **Activating Spiritual Gifts**

C. **Manifestation of Gifts**
    1. Gifts of Revelation
        a. Word of Wisdom
        b. Word of Knowledge
        c. Discerning of Spirits
    2. Gifts of Power
        a. Gift of Faith
        b. Gifts of Healing
        c. Working of Miracles
    3. Gifts of Inspiration
        a. Gift of Prophecy
        b. Gift of Tongues
        c. Interpretation of Tongues
    4. Motivational Gifts
    5. Ministry Gifts

D. **Discovering Spiritual Gifts**

E. **Results of Activating Spiritual Gifts**
    1. Satisfaction
    2. Edification
    3. Glorification

Book Four

I Am Supernatural
Walking in Spiritual Gifts
Introduction

As a believer, the Holy Spirit gave you special gifts designed for edifying and encouraging the saints and building up the church. The Greek word for 'gift' is *charisma*, which is where Christianity gets the term charismatic, which describes things done through the power of the Holy Spirit. The root word *'charis'* means grace. Therefore, you receive the gifts of the Holy Spirit through the grace of God. Spiritual gifts are not earnable; they are not rewards nor do you deserve them. They are gifts! The Holy Spirit decides what gift or gifts to give you, according to the unique purpose He has ordained for your life.

Understanding Spiritual Gifts

What are Spiritual Gifts? Spiritual gifts are supernatural abilities given through the Holy Spirit. As noted, you don't deserve them and you can't earn them. The Holy Spirit gives gifts through His power. Spiritual gifts differ from the gift of the Holy Spirit. There is only one Holy Spirit given to you. There are multiple spiritual gifts given to you by the Holy Spirit. The distribution of spiritual gifts was given by Christ when He ascended to heaven because of the love Jesus has for His people. Spiritual gifts are not the same as the Fruit of the Spirit. I heard it once said that gifts are the means and fruit is the result. Fruit of the Spirit and spiritual gifts work together and complement each other, but are different in their descriptions.

Spiritual gifts enable you to do effective work that glorifies God and advances the cause of Christ. Spiritual gifts are not to put you on a pedestal. They are given to draw others to Christ so they may gain freedom from sin, live in the blessing of Christ, and minister to others on behalf of Christ.

"Therefore He says: "When He ascended on high, He led captivity captive, and gave gifts to men."(Now this, "He ascended"—what does it mean but that

He also first descended into the lower parts of the earth? He who descended is also the One who ascended far above all the heavens, that He might fill all things.) And He Himself gave some to be apostles, some prophets, some evangelists, and some pastors and teachers, for the equipping of the saints for the work of ministry, for the edifying of the body of Christ" Ephesians 4:8-12.

Purpose of Spiritual Gifts

Spiritual gifts 'build up' the church. We are not talking about building a building called a church. We are talking about encouraging and edifying individuals who also believe in Jesus, sometimes called brothers and sisters in Christ. To 'build up' something means to prepare it for a significant event or to increase it. The purpose of spiritual gifts is to help Christians be victorious over sin and become more like Jesus. Gifts prepare Christians for eternity.

The gifts equip believers in Christ with the ability to fulfill a God-given task. Throughout your life, there will be many opportunities or divine appointments prepared by God where the Holy Spirit can use the gifts He gave you to help other people. By yourself, you probably wouldn't even notice those opportunities and would rarely do them without God on your side. Because of the gifts in you, not only can you see those opportunities but also fulfill your divine destiny while helping others walk out their destiny.

SPIRITUAL GIFTS AND TALENTS

In addition to Spiritual Gifts, God also gives talents. Talents and spiritual gifts are alike in some ways and different in other ways. Both will grow in effectiveness when they are practiced and developed. Both benefit others, not ourselves. Talents are often inherited while spiritual gifts are received. A talent is a natural genetic propensity to do a certain thing or learn something specific. Musical talent is a great example of a talent that can be passed on to children through genetics. Spiritual gifts are supernatural endowments.

Anyone, saved or unsaved, believers and unbelievers, can have talent. Since talents come through natural means, anyone can possess and develop their talent. Spiritual gifts belong to believers or Christians. Since Jesus gave spiritual gifts to believers and the gifts work through the Holy Spirit, it is God's children who function supernaturally in the spiritual gifts.

Talent may be a combination of genetics and training and/or a special endowment from God. Talents usually don't just happen except in the rare prodigy. Talents often take a combination of genetics and training to develop, but even without genetics, a talent can become more fine-tuned with training and use. If you have genetically received the ability to learn certain things, then training can increase that talent. Since talents are natural, talents benefit man on a natural level. You may enjoy a great song, a beautiful painting, a skilled sports talent, an excellent architectural design, a well-written book, a great suit design, a fantastic haircut, and many other amazing talents. Look around you. Everything you see came from someone's talent or gift. You need people's talents and probably enjoy many people's talents. Talents help in so many ways it's too innumerable to list.

Though talents are part of the natural part of life, God will still use them. God can empower a person with a certain talent at a certain time for a specific purpose, anointing that talent for a purpose. There is an account in Exodus where the Lord gave certain people specific abilities to complete the building of the tabernacle. Whether their skills were talents or gifts is not specified, but we do know they were gifted and filled with the Spirit of God for the specific purpose of building the tabernacle according to God's design. So what happens with your gifts and talents when the Spirit of God fills you? Amazing things happen.

"Then the Lord spoke to Moses, saying: "See, I have called by name Bezalel the son of Uri, the son of Hur, of the tribe of Judah. And I have filled him with the Spirit of God, in wisdom, in understanding, in knowledge, and in all manner of workmanship, to design artistic works, to work in gold, in silver, in bronze, in cutting jewels for setting, in carving wood, and to work in all manner of workmanship. "And I, indeed I, have appointed with him Aholiab the son of Ahisamach, of the tribe of Dan; and I have put wisdom in the hearts of all the gifted artisans, that they may make all that I have commanded you," Exodus 31:1-6.

Activating Spiritual Gifts

Once you receive your spiritual gift/s, you must **ACTIVATE YOUR GIFT** or gifts. Activating your spiritual gifts requires something from you. It requires faith and putting your feet to your faith. B that you have spiritual gifts and practice using them. Perhaps you have the gift of healing. Then, pray for people who need healing and believe that the Lord has healed them. We will talk more in-depth on this as we talk about the gifts. The enemy wants you to think you don't have any gifts. Even your mind will tell you that you aren't worthy to have God's gifts or that God wouldn't give gifts to someone 'like you.' Those are lies to keep you from flowing or moving in your gifts. God freely gives you the gifts of the Spirit. What if you see a gift you want but don't think you have it? It's okay to ask for them if you don't see them in your life. You can even pursue the gifts of the Spirit. So if there is a spiritual gift you do not see in your life, just ask God for it. He will gladly give gifts to you or show you the ones you already have. He even tells you to desire them!

"But earnestly desire the best gifts... Pursue love, and desire spiritual gifts, but especially that you may prophesy," 1 Corinthians 12:31; 14:1.

Another way of activating spiritual gifts in your life is by a practice called the laying on of hands. Laying on of hands is pretty much just

19

what it sounds like. A person of authority in Christianity such as a pastor, prophet, teacher, or minister will touch you with their hands and pray to activate the gifts. Hands will usually touch your head or hands or perhaps your shoulders. It will always be appropriate and in order. Spiritual gifts can be instantly activated through the laying on of hands. Timothy was a young pastor in the New Testament. The gift of being a pastor was activated in him by elders in Christianity through the laying on of hands.

"Do not neglect the gift that is in you, which was given to you by prophecy with the laying on of the hands of the eldership," 1 Timothy 4:14.

The Word of God is essential in activating spiritual gifts. Actively reading and meditating on the Scriptures is necessary for spiritual gifts to operate effectively. An active prayer life is important so you can learn to hear the direction of the Holy Spirit and increase your wisdom and understanding. Hiding the Word of God in your heart provides a solid foundation from which spiritual gifts can flow. The spiritual gifts will not be effective or operate according to God's will if scripture and prayer are not in the recipe.

Manifestation or Expression of Spiritual Gifts

The gifts of the Spirit are God's gift to the body of Christ. They are gifts given by God to His children. Gifts cannot be earned, nor are they purchased. They are freely given to you for the edification and encouragement of fellow believers. Following are the Spiritual Gifts according to 1 Corinthians 12:1-11.

"Now concerning spiritual gifts, brethren, I do not want you to be ignorant: You know that you were Gentiles, carried away to these dumb idols, however you were led. Therefore, I make known to you that no one speaking by the Spirit of God calls Jesus accursed, and no one can say that Jesus is Lord except by the Holy Spirit. There are diversities of gifts, but the same Spirit. There are differences of ministries, but the same Lord. And there are diversities of activities, but it is the same God who works all in all. But the manifestation of the Spirit is given to each one for the profit of all: for to one is given the word of wisdom through the Spirit, to another the word of knowledge through the same Spirit, to another faith by the same Spirit, to another gifts of healings by the same Spirit, to another the working of miracles, to another prophecy, to another discerning of spirits, to another different kinds of tongues, to another the interpretation of tongues. But one and the same Spirit works all these things, distributing to each one individually as He wills."

Gifts of Revelation

The gifts of revelation are used to reveal information to a person outside of natural means of communication. The information is not something you read in a book or reasoned or analyzed from what you already learned, saw, or heard. It's a divine revelation from heaven of facts that are unknown by prior knowledge. Gifts of revelation include Word of Wisdom, Word of Knowledge, and Discerning of Spirits.

WORD OF WISDOM

Word of wisdom is the supernatural revelation of the divine will of God, specifically events that have not yet occurred or are of the future. It's **GOD'S PERSPECTIVE** on a situation. Word of wisdom is a supernatural revelation or disclosure of the divine will of God. You cannot know it through books or education or gossip or the internet or any natural means. You only know a word of wisdom through the supernatural power of the Holy Spirit. A word of wisdom enables the believer to make sound decisions because of insightful perception. Humans make decisions with selfish intentions or from a logical/reasoning perspective. With a word of wisdom, you can make decisions that consider others with insight into

23

the results of your decisions. A word of wisdom is supernatural intelligence that uses skill and prudence to deliver the truth. You can study all the books in the universe and still not have the wisdom that God can give you supernaturally. It is a deep insight into the holiness of God and the lack of holiness in you or someone else. Along with that insight comes the compassion to offer that truth with empathy and kindness.

An example of the Word of Wisdom in the Bible is when Joseph was asked to interpret dreams. Joseph not only gave the meaning of the dreams but also provided a way for the kingdom of Egypt to survive and prosper during a coming famine. Pharaoh was dreaming about cows—fat ones and skinny ones. The dream troubled him, but none of his magicians could interpret the dream. He heard about Joseph and called him to the palace, asking Joseph to interpret the dream. Joseph told Pharaoh, 'Oh no Pharaoh, it's God that interprets not me!' God showed Joseph what the dream meant. Joseph told Pharaoh and as a result, Egypt survived a famine not only protecting its nation but helping neighboring people, prospering in the midst of what could have been devastation. Not only that, but Joseph who was a prisoner at the time of this dream became the second most powerful man in Egypt. The word of wisdom God gave him prospered so many and got Joseph out of prison and into the palace. I encourage you to read the full account of this story in Genesis 41.

WORD OF KNOWLEDGE

Word of Knowledge does not come from your intelligence or academic knowledge. This knowledge is not about what you know. Word of Knowledge is the insight of the Holy Spirit. It is information that there is no way you could know without the Spirit of God. Word of Knowledge is specific knowledge to an individual about something you would have no ability or means to know. The Word of Knowledge given to someone enables them to better understand or know how to deal with situations in their life. A Word of Knowledge focuses on that which exists, whether in times past or the present. It's a gift related to facts. A Word of Knowledge is used to deliver a message to someone. It's saying the right thing at the right time to the right person for the right purpose, which can only occur with the insight of the Holy Spirit. It is an opening to deliver a truth that the Holy Spirit would like revealed at the most opportune moment.

An example of a Word of Knowledge is when Jesus was sitting at a well in Samaria in the middle of the day. A woman approached the well and had a conversation with this stranger resting by the well. During their conversation, Jesus, who had never met the woman before and had no natural way of knowing anything about her, told her how many husbands she had in the past and that the man she currently lived with was not her husband. Through that expression of knowledge, the woman opened her heart to Jesus, received the truth about the Messiah, then went and told everyone in the village! Because of the Word of Knowledge given to an outcast woman, her life completely changed as she drank living water from the truth Jesus expounded to her. As a result, an entire village was offered an opportunity to receive the gospel truth. The Samaritan woman's story is found in John 4.

DISCERNING OF SPIRITS

Discerning of Spirits is a divine supernatural ability to see into the spirit realm to detect and reveal hidden intentions, whether good or evil. You want to **DISCERN SPIRITS SO YOU WON'T BE DECEIVED** or tricked to do or think things that are against God's will and ways. Discerning of Spirits test the spirits in the world to see if they are of God or of another. 1 John tells a little about different spirits and instructs to test them, so you know their origin.

"Beloved, do not believe every spirit, but test the spirits, whether they are of God; because many false prophets have gone out into the world. By this you know the Spirit of God: Every spirit that confesses that Jesus Christ has come in the flesh is of God, and every spirit that does not confess that Jesus Christ has come in the flesh is not of God. And this is the spirit of the Antichrist, which you have heard was coming, and is now already in the world. You are of God, little children, and have overcome them, because He who is in you is greater than he who is in the world," 1 John 4:1-4.

There are three different types of spirits besides the Holy Spirit that can be discerned or recognized: demonic spirits, heavenly spirits, and human spirits. Demonic spirits are fallen angels. When the angel, Lucifer (satan), rebelled against God and was expelled from heaven, he took one-third of heaven's angels with him. They began waging war on God. Because you belong to God's family, he wages war on you, too. These **demonic spirits** come to kill, steal, and destroy. Their every intent comes from rebellion and destruction. Sometimes, whatever they are bringing might look amazing, but no matter how compelling their enticement, it will always lead to destruction. We will talk more about these spirits in the *I Am Strong* book in the *Walking with Jesus* series.

"So the great dragon was cast out, that serpent of old, called the Devil and Satan, who deceives the whole world; he was cast to the earth, and his angels were cast out with him" Revelation 12:9.

26

Other spirits are God's angels who are **heavenly spirits**. Angels have great power. They have a rank much like military rank, and they have different jobs. Angels were not created to serve humans as some would believe. They were created to serve God. Angels are not glorified humans like the movies want you to believe. There is an old show that was on TV called *Highway to Heaven*. It was about this man who passed away, became a probationary angel, was sent to earth to help people in need until he earned his way into heaven. It was a clean, family-friendly show, but far from the truth. Heavenly angels are individuals just like you and me. You don't earn your way to heaven as a probationary angel. Bells don't mean some dead person earned their angel wings like Clarence did on the Christmas classic film *It's a Wonderful Life*. Angels are beings that minister to God and minister to His people, including bringing messages from God.

"Are they not all ministering spirits sent forth to minister for those who will inherit salvation?" Hebrews 1:14.

"Behold, an angel of the Lord appeared to Joseph in a dream," Matthew 2:13.

Man is a three-part being—body, soul, and spirit. The **human spirit** is the part of a person that can connect with God. It is God-consciousness. Because of the fall of man and sin, the human spirit is damaged. Sin brings death to the human spirit. That's why you need God to breathe life into you. The human spirit is made in the image of God and is made alive with the breath of God when a person accepts Christ into their life. God's Spirit speaks to the human spirit. The human spirit has its own set of emotions, passions, creativity, and intellect that respond to God and that differs from your body's emotions, passions, creativity, and intellect.

The gift of discerning of spirits has an insight into which spirit is which. You need the ability to tell the difference because there are spirits that are very cunning and skilled at deception and trickery. God's children need the ability to see into the spiritual realm and discern the spirits. Discerning of spirits is definitely a supernatural superpower. It is very important to have a strong biblical foundation to operate effectively in this gift. Jesus was operating in discernment when His beloved disciple, Peter, was talking to him. Jesus saw the man, and just as importantly, He saw the spirit working behind the words that were spoken. Instead of answering Peter, Jesus spoke directly to the spirit telling it to get behind Him.

Gifts of Power

Power gifts fill you with a supernatural ability that you cannot naturally possess. The power gifts operate in harmony; one does not manifest without the presence of the others. The power gifts are faith, healing, and the working of miracles. These gifts are a trio of superpowers that bring God glory, draw people to Jesus, and bless you tremendously.

Gift of Faith

The gift of faith is the divine ability to accomplish a task without the involvement of your strengths. God's power infuses you with supernatural confidence, presence, and promises. The gift of faith solely relies on the power of God and not anything a person can do. Supernatural faith instills confidence in the power and promises of God as unshakable, immovable, and strong. The gift of faith provides a **SUPERNATURAL ABILITY** to supply a specific need. Noah had faith and built an ark. Through faith, Abraham believed God and inherited a land of promise. By faith, Sarah, who was nearly a hundred years old conceived and had a baby boy. Moses through faith delivered a nation from slavery. The list is long of those who supernaturally left a significant footprint in history through the gift of faith. I encourage you to read more about people who walked in this kind of faith in Hebrews 11, which is known as the hall of faith chapter.

"Now faith is the substance of things hoped for, the evidence of things not seen. For by it the elders obtained a good testimony. By faith we understand that the worlds were framed by the word of God, so that the things which are seen were not made of things which are visible," Hebrews 11:1-2.

You already function on some levels of faith. You have natural faith, which is based on works. Farmers show an example of natural faith. They plant a field with a few seeds of corn and believe that it will yield a harvest of corn. You have faith that gravity will hold you on the earth. You mail a letter and have faith the postal system will get it where it needs to go. Sometimes people refer to this faith as common sense, a natural way of perceiving things. You need natural faith to function in the world. You and every person on the planet have saving faith. Saving faith is activated when you hear the Word of God, believe it, and accept Jesus Christ as Lord and Savior. Saving faith is the instrument God uses to bring you to salvation and a belief in the Savior. It's a gift given to you through grace. You need saving faith to step into the spiritual world.

Natural faith and saving faith differ from the gift of faith. The gift of faith is not based on your ability, natural events, or anything a person can do. It results from God's abilities—supernatural. The gift of faith is a superpower that lets you l**OOK BEYOND THE REALITY OF YOUR TODAY AND REALIZE YOUR DREAMS AND HOPES.** Look at Noah. (You can read Noah's story in Genesis 6-9.) He looked beyond the reality of his today and saw an ark. Noah lived in a world that was corrupt and violent. He had faith the ark was needed because of floodwater. Now that's a big vision! I can imagine if I was Noah asking 'well what's an ark and how could there be enough water to flood a desert or mountains and destroy the whole earth?' But Noah didn't question God. He simply believed what he was told and obeyed God's commanded, and saved humanity. That's the gift of faith.

Gifts of Healing

The gifts of healing are the only gift of the nine spiritual gifts that is written in plural form. To function in the gifts of healing, have faith that God's will is to heal, and that He has the power to heal. The International Classification of Disease, ninth revision (ICD-9) classifies thirty-nine disease categories. Though there are thousands of diseases, they are coded into thirty-nine categories. After Jesus was arrested and before the crucifixion, the authorities delivered a brutal thrashing upon His body. They whipped Jesus thirty-nine times, leaving thirty-nine fiendish, bleeding stripes across His body that tore His flesh so He was unrecognizable. He endured those thirty-nine lashes for a reason. Each of those thirty-nine disease categories in this world was healed with each one of those thirty-nine lashes. No disease is unhealable. Jesus made sure of that.

"But He was wounded for our transgressions, He was bruised for our iniquities; the chastisement for our peace was upon Him, and by His stripes we are healed," Isaiah 53:5.

The gifts of healing are used to heal disease, sickness, illness, and disorders. They bring deliverance and so much more. The gifts of healing reveal the compassion and heart of God. He desires to see you healed and whole. The gift of healing can be transmitted through different means. The gift of healing can transpire through prayer. You can pray for yourself or someone else and release God's healing power. The laying on of hands is another way to minister the gifts of healing. Often anointing oil will be used when laying hands on an individual and praying for their healing. You can even anoint yourself with oil. Anointing oil was used in the Scriptures as a representation of the presence of the Holy Spirit and the need for the power of God for healing. The gifts of healing can occur through natural means—physicians and medicine, especially when prayer is involved.

"Is anyone among you sick? Let him call for the elders of the church, and let them pray over him, anointing him with oil in the name of the Lord. And the prayer of faith will save the sick, and the Lord will raise him up. And if he has committed sins, he will be forgiven," James 5:14-15.

However, it is important to remember that the gifts of healing are always to exalt God, bring Him glory, and edifying and encouraging people. None of the gifts are to bring any individual recognition. Look at Peter in Acts 5. His gifts of healings were so powerful that people brought their sick out to the streets just so Peter's shadow would fall on them and heal them. Many, many people were healed and Peter didn't even touch them or individually pray for them. His faith was so strong and his confidence in the healing power of God so mighty that it sparked faith in the sick and those who loved them so much so that all it took was Peter's shadow to fall on them to complete their healing.

"And believers were increasingly added to the Lord, multitudes of both men and women, so that they brought the sick out into the streets and laid them on beds and couches, that at least the shadow of Peter passing by might fall on some of them. Also, a multitude gathered from the surrounding cities to Jerusalem, bringing sick people and those who were tormented by unclean spirits, and they were all healed," Acts 5:14-17.

We will not all have shadow-healing ministries, but you certainly can flow in the gifts of healing. I heard an account of the plumber/preacher Smith Wigglesworth and how one specific healing took place under his ministry. He went to a person's house to fix their plumbing and found out they were severely ill. He took a moment to ask the Lord how to minister healing to them. The answer was to slap them and speak specific words, which the Lord gave him. SLAP them! Wigglesworth did exactly that. He slapped the person and spoke the word that the Lord gave him. That person was stunned initially and then it sparked faith so much in that person that they were completely healed of an unhealable disease at that exact moment. You can minister healing in many ways. That's why there are gifts not just one gift of healings. Different healing might need a different gift. Speaking God's Word releases healing powers. The Word of God is powerful. When you speak the Word over health issues, healing is the result.

"He sent His word and healed them, and delivered them from their destructions," Psalm 107:20 KJV.

WORKING OF MIRACLES

Working of miracles is a supernatural occurrence that goes beyond natural abilities and comprehension. You can only go so far in your natural existence. You can only comprehend things of this world. With the power of God's spiritual gift of miracles, you can go beyond your natural abilities and comprehend things beyond your natural intelligence. Miracles are the Spirit of God working through you to perform extraordinary tasks. Jesus performed a miracle when He turned water into wine and when He fed 5,000 men plus their families with five loaves of bread and two fishes. Moses did a miracle when he raised his staff and the Red Sea parted, allowing the people of Israel to escape from Egyptian slavery. None of those are possible except through miracles.

Miracles are an intervention of God in the natural world. Peter walked on the water with Jesus. Daniel stayed an entire night in a den of starving lions without being eaten. The natural world is subject to the power of God. He can intervene in the natural universe anytime. Working of miracles will alter the laws of nature and natural reasoning. Miracles rarely make sense. They boggle your mind. They can perplex and disorient, but they will always reveal God to His people.

"Jesus said to them, "Fill the waterpots with water." And they filled them up to the brim. And He said to them, "Draw some out now, and take it to the master of the feast." And they took it. When the master of the feast had tasted the water that was made wine, and did not know where it came from (but the servants who had drawn the water knew), the master of the feast called the bridegroom," John 2:7-9.

I will not dwell on the working of miracles because the topic is so vast and wide. What you need to know is that the gift of working of miracles is real. Miracles still happen today. God probably has a miracle in motion for you right now! You can't conjure up a miracle. They happen according to the will of God and faith. Do you see why these three power gifts work together? Healing requires faith and may just require a miracle. Miracles require faith and might just bring a lot of healing to many people in a lot of ways. The three are so closely tied and intertwined that it's nearly impossible to separate them.

Gifts of Inspiration

The gifts of utterance, expression, or inspiration are designed to encourage and strengthen the people of Christ. These gifts primarily involve corporate worship as exhortation, edification, and comfort. Corporate worship is when believers get together to honor God. This may be in a church setting, someone's home, or just about anywhere. Exhortation is God's form of encouragement. Edification is God's enlightenment, and comfort is much needed in a world of strife and turmoil.

"But he who prophesies speaks edification and exhortation and comfort to men. He who speaks in a tongue edifies himself, but he who prophesies edifies the church. I wish you all spoke with tongues, but even more that you prophesied; he who prophesies is greater than he who speaks with tongues, unless indeed he interprets, that the church may receive edification," 1 Corinthians 14:3-5.

GIFT OF PROPHECY

The gift of prophecy is a supernatural utterance or statement given through one of God's people. Prophecy is intended to encourage, inspire, and comfort those who hear the divinely inspired message. A prophecy may include a special message from God or foretelling of the divine will for an individual or God's people. It may bring correction, reveal secret sins, and expose wrong attitudes. **PROPHECY WILL EXPOSE TRUE MOTIVES.** It isn't about condemning for wrongs or predicting the future. It's about helping individuals develop a heart of purity and holiness. Prophecy may be about future events or give revelation (disclosure) of God's equipping to fulfill destiny. Prophetic messages can come in many forms. One form of prophecy is someone speaking a prophecy. Prophecy can come through the voice of an angel, in a dream or a vision. God sends messages straight from His heart to help His church grow. Prophecy will build up areas of weakness in character or spirit. It will encourage a lifestyle of holiness and console in the face of sorrow. Prophecy will never go against the Word of God. The gift of prophecy can work through anyone and is not limited to pastors or people who hold the office of prophet. A child can prophesy. You can prophesy. Sensitivity to the Holy Spirit will help discern between prophecy and someone's opinions. Prophecies foretold when and where Jesus would be born, how He would die, and that His resurrection would change lives. Prophecies told about the captivity of Israel and their deliverance. The Book of Revelation in the New Testament is filled with prophecy about the future of God's people.

There is a difference between holding the office of a prophet and the gift of prophecy. We will talk about the prophetic office in the *Ministry Gifts* chapter.

"He that prophesies edifies the church," 1 Corinthians 14:4b.

Remember, this is a gift of the Holy Spirit. It isn't a 'this is what I think about that' or 'this is what I want to happen' speech. Prophecy comes from the heart of God through the Holy Spirit and will never go against the will of God. Scripture supports prophecy. Those 'prophecies' where someone tells you to leave your spouse because someone else is your true mate are lying prophecies. I love how the gifts of the spirit work together. You need the gift of discernment to tell which prophecies are true and which are lies. You need the gift of faith to believe what God is telling you and to put it into action. And God gives you all that and more! Isn't it beautiful?

GIFT OF TONGUES

The spiritual gift of tongues is not the ability to speak in various languages. You don't have to be a linguist to have the gifts of various tongues. It is not a language you learned in any class. The gift of tongues is a language straight from heaven. It is a supernatural communication that comes from God through the Holy Spirit and uses your ability to speak. The gift of tongues was released after Jesus ascended to heaven. This gift was first demonstrated on the Day of Pentecost. The gift of tongues is a sign of God's presence in your life.

"And these signs shall follow them that believe; in my name shall they cast out devils; they shall speak with new tongues," Mark 16:17.

Tongues manifest in a spiritual language with no connection to the natural mind. As you speak this spiritual language, it is possible you will not know what is being communicated. However, others may understand. You are not speaking gibberish. In Acts, the disciples were speaking languages they did not understand, but some who could hear knew exactly what was being said. Speaking in tongues is **SPEECH DIRECTED BY GOD**. It is different from your spiritual prayer language. When you are filled with the Spirit of God, He gives you a private, special language that is shared between only you and You're your special prayer language may sound to you much the same as speaking in tongues, however, it is very different. Your prayer language is between you and God in privacy. Speaking in tongues generally happens publicly. It occurs in public settings such as a worship service. When the disciples were speaking in tongues, in Acts 2, people heard unlearned men speaking in languages they shouldn't have known but were speaking fluently. While your private prayer language is communication between you and God, speaking in tongues communicates the gospel to those in the hearing of the one speaking and confirms the gospel message.

"And they were all filled with the Holy Spirit and began to speak with other tongues, as the Spirit gave them utterance. And there were dwelling in Jerusalem Jews, devout men, from every nation under heaven. And when this sound occurred, the multitude came together, and were confused, because everyone heard them speak in his own language. Then they were all amazed and marveled," Acts 2:4-7.

When the Lord gives a message to speak in tongues, it should always be subject to the person in authority. For instance, your message in tongues should not interrupt a pastor while delivering his message. To randomly shout out a message in tongues is not in God's order. It takes discipline to give a message in tongues at the proper moment since the unction to speak the message can be quite strong. Operating in the **GIFT OF TONGUES REQUIRES FAITH** since you are speaking words you do not understand and trusting God to minister to others through those words.

"For he who speaks in a tongue does not speak to men but to God, for no one understands him; however, in the spirit he speaks mysteries... For if I pray in a tongue, my spirit prays, but my understanding is unfruitful," 1 Corinthians 14:2, 14.

Interpretation of Tongues

The interpretation of tongues is the **SUPERNATURAL ABILITY** to interpret a message of an unknown tongue or language. Whenever someone
releases the gift of tongues in a church service or during a gospel teaching, the Word states that to be decent and in order, there will always be
an interpretation of the message that went forth with the gift of tongues.
The interpretation of tongues is not a translation. A translation is a word-
for-word rendering of a message from one language to another. In con-
trast, an interpretation reveals the understanding of the message God has
delivered in paraphrased form. The gift of tongues and the interpretation
of tongues are not connected to the natural mind. The mind cannot understand the spiritual language. Therefore, it requires faith to operate in
this gift. When the gift of interpretation flows with its counterpart gift,
the gift of tongues, people will experience edification, enlightenment,
encouragement, comfort, and faith increases.

*"And when the day of Pentecost was fully come, they were all with one
accord in one place. And suddenly there came a sound from heaven as of a
rushing mighty wind, and it filled all the house where they were sitting. And
there appeared unto them cloven tongues like as of fire, and it sat upon each of
them. And they were all filled with the Holy Ghost, and began to speak with
other tongues, as the Spirit gave them utterance. And there were dwelling at
Jerusalem Jews, devout men, out of every nation under heaven. Now when
this was noised abroad, the multitude came together, and were confounded,
because that every man heard them speak in his own language. And they
were all amazed and marveled, saying one to another, Behold, are not all
these which speak Galileans? And how hear we every man in our own tongue,
wherein we were born? Parthians, and Medes, and Elamites, and the dwell-*

ers in Mesopotamia, and in Judaea, and Cappadocia, in Pontus, and Asia, Phrygia, and Pamphylia, in Egypt, and in the parts of Libya about Cyrene, and strangers of Rome, Jews and proselytes, Cretes and Arabians, we do hear them speak in our tongues the wonderful works of God. And they were all amazed," Acts 2:1-12 KJV.

Motivational Gifts

God is not stingy with His gifts. The nine spiritual gifts are not the only gifts given to believers. God gave additional gifts to the Body of Christ to further advance His kingdom on earth. There are many gifts. Here are a few:

- **Gift of Helps**. Helps is the investment of your talents and abilities into the work of God, thus helping to increase the effectiveness of ministry work. This may come in many forms. Helps is often a behind-the-scenes service and those who labor in Helps often labor in obscurity. The Ministry of Helps is the ministry of 'lending a hand'. Examples of the ministry of Helps are those who volunteer to mow a yard, clean the church, deliver a meal, or serve those in need. It is probably the most anonymous gift and one of the most important because it touches people at their basic need.

- **Gift of exhortation**. The gift of exhortation is the ability to minister words of encouragement, comfort, and consolation in a way that offers support and healing. It is a gift of encouragement that brings strength to someone who needs an inspirational boost. It isn't about building someone's ego, but about reinforcing who they are in Christ.

- **Gift of administration**. The gift of administration enables you to devise and execute immediate and long-range goals effectively within the body of Christ. If you have the gift of administration, you organize, plan, and implement projects, lead people, manage finances and information. Those with the gift of administration are often strategic thinkers, and their organizational skills are impeccable. Attention to detail usually accompanies this gift as well as the ability to make decisions.

- **Gift of giving**. The gift of giving is more than being able to give something to someone. It isn't about buying your nephew a birthday present. The gift of giving is a divine ability to give sincerely, generously, without hypocrisy, and expecting nothing in return. The gift of giving is used to meet the various needs of the church and its ministries. People with this gift love to share with others what God has given them. They are excellent stewards of their blessings and usually very hospitable. When someone willfully contributes their resource to God's works with cheerfulness and liberty, they are using the gift of giving. Joy encompasses them like a halo.

- **Gift of mercy**. The gift of mercy is the ability to empathize and be compassionate on behalf of people. The gift of mercy manifests or is visible in concern for the physical and spiritual needs of those who are hurting, to bear one another's burdens, to be sensitive to the feelings and circumstances of others. Often those with the gift of mercy are good listeners and want to help others however they can. They are motivated by others' needs and respond with kindness and gentleness. Distress is like a magnet. They see someone in distress and must help. People with the gift of mercy touch others, often at the very point of their hurts and fears.

- **Gift of leadership**. The gift of leadership is the gift of discerning the purpose for a group, communicate the goals, and motivate others to accomplish those goals. This gift governs situations. Those with the gift of leadership understand that Christ is the head of everything and that His people are His servants. The gift of leadership helps the church grow and thrive. They do not take glory for themselves in their accomplishments but acknowledge that God is the one to glorify. The Bible has many examples of humble yet powerful leaders—Moses, David, Paul, and many more.

Ministry Gifts

There is another set of gifts that the Bible lists besides those we have already discussed. They are often called the fivefold ministry gifts. The ministry gifts are leadership roles within the church. God gives the fivefold ministry gifts to the body of Christ to advance the Kingdom of God on earth. They work together for the edification, enlightenment, and teaching of the church and to prepare God's people for the works of service in ministry.

"And he gave some, apostles; and some, prophets; and some, evangelists; and some, pastors and teachers; for the perfecting of the saints, unto the work of ministry, for the building up of the body of Christ," Ephesians 4:11-12 KJV.

- **Apostle** is one sent with a **SPECIAL COMMISSION** from Jesus Christ to govern the church. Any person with an apostolic calling has the ability, authority, and anointing to build and establish a church. They lay spiritual foundations for a church and see that it comes into maturity in Christ. Apostles carry the burden to establish a church in strong biblical teaching. They train church leaders to grow and mature so they can also go out and build new churches.

Apostles create disciples through their teaching and leadership. The apostle differs from the other four offices in that an apostle can function in the other four roles - pastor, evangelist, teacher, or prophet - as needed. An example of an apostle is the Apostle Paul, who was used mightily to build the early church. God, not man, chose him to work on behalf of the church. Some say there are no more apostles since the original apostles from the first century. Perhaps there are no more apostles that hold that specific office of Apostle. However, the gift of the apostle did not end with the original apostles. The gift is not only still in operation today, but important in the building and maturity of the church.

"Paul, an apostle, (not of men, neither by man, but by Jesus Christ, and God the Father, who raised him from the dead)" Galatians 1:1 KJV.

- God appoints the office of prophet to bring **PROPHETIC REVELA-TION** from God to the body of Christ. You and I can prophesy, but that doesn't mean we are prophets. Every Christian, when you are in communication with God, can receive a word from Him to share with someone. Prophets don't just sometimes deliver a prophetic message. Their job or office is to prophesy. Prophecy encourages, comforts, reproves, and has a passionate sense of justice. Prophecy can foretell events and provide in-depth insight into God's Word. Prophets are not fortunetellers. They don't create futuristic information for you. Prophets don't sugarcoat the message they are to deliver or adjust to meet your needs. They tell the message of God, even if it causes them distress or problems. Often prophecy is a **WAKE-UP** call. Prophecy will not go against scripture or God's will. Prophets bring messages that guide, give revelation and understanding, provide timing, and help with understanding how to apply biblical truths.

Isaiah is an example of someone who held the office of prophet. He denounced Judah's disobedient religious practices, predicted the nation's deliverance from captivity, and even predicted certain events of Jesus' life.

"And we have the word of the prophets made more certain, and you will do well to pay attention to it, as to a light shining in a dark place, until the day dawns and the morning star rises in your hearts" 2 Peter 1:19 NIV.

- An **evangelist** is one who proclaims the gospel of Jesus Christ to those who have not yet accepted Jesus into their lives and joined the body of Christ. God anoints evangelists to preach the Gospel with a great conviction to share the message of Christ to those who do not yet know the Lord. Evangelists enjoy direct contact with people. They may deliver their message one-on-one or in mass assemblies. **SIGNS AND WONDERS** often follow evangelists to confirm their message. One of their principal missions is to bring the Gospel to people to help them understand Jesus and salvation. The Spirit anoints evangelists to impart God's heart toward those who are lost.

John the Baptist is an example of one who preaches the message of Christ.

"The next day John saw Jesus coming toward him and said, "Look, the Lamb of God, who takes away the sin of the world!" John 1:29 NIV.

- **Pastors** are shepherds of the body of believers. Pastors have a heart for serving. They are the guardians of God's people. The mark of a true pastor is their heart's connection to the sheep, the people of God. A pastor wants to feed his flock so they grow strong. He equips the people and helps them to develop their gifts and fulfill their calling in Christ. The ministry of a pastor is to feed the flock with knowledge and understanding of the Word of God. Pastors care for the day-to-day needs of the people. They live through the everyday events, struggles, and joys of the church people. Pastors train, teach, correct, and protect.

The Bible calls Jesus the "**GOOD SHEPHERD.**" He is an example of how a pastor cares for the people of God with love.

"I am the good shepherd. The good shepherd gives His life for the sheep. But a hireling, he who is not the shepherd, one who does not own the sheep, sees the wolf coming and leaves the sheep and flees; and the wolf catches the sheep and scatters them" John 10:11-12.

- **Teacher** feeds spiritual truth to believers to develop Christian maturity. They can communicate Biblical truth in such a way that it is easy for others to learn. Teachers reveal hidden truths in the Word of God with insight. Teachers communicate how to apply the Scriptures to daily living. There is an old warning not to be so spiritually minded that you are no earthly good. The book of James also warns not to be caught in the things of the world like fighting, gossiping, adultery, and a long list of other worldly devices. Teachers of the Scriptures and the Truth of God bring balance to everyday life.

God called Moses to teach the people of Israel. The following scripture was directed at Moses but is true for today's teachers as well.

"Teach them the decrees and laws, and show them the way to live and the duties they are to perform," Exodus 18:20 NIV.

Discovering Spiritual Gifts

God gives everyone at least one spiritual gift, and you probably have more than one. You may already know what your spiritual gift is, or you may still wonder where you fit and what gifts you bring to the family of God. We have listed many of the gifts mentioned in the Bible, but there are so many opportunities that we can't talk about all of them. There are some actions you can take to help you discover your spiritual gifts. Here a few things you can do:

- **Ask God.** This may be the simplest thing to do. God loves you and desires that you find your purpose and destiny in life. Your gift/s have been given to you to help others find their purpose and destiny in life. God will be happy to show you your gift. Just ask Him. Don't forget to listen for the answer.

- **Be aware.** As you study the Word and watch other believers, you will see their gifts, which will help you see your own. As you understand the different gifts and see them function in the church, you will begin to see gifts similar to your gifts which will help you discover how to use your gifts.

- **Desire spiritual gifts.** What do you want to do? Find a gift you desire to fulfill and present it to God. If you have a sincere desire to use a particular gift, God can develop a gift in you and provide opportunities to use that gift.

- **Actively try.** If you aren't sure what your spiritual gifts are, then try out some different things. Volunteer. Explore different options. If it doesn't fit, don't wear it!

- **Aptitude**. There are several Spiritual Gift assessments you can take to better help you understand the gift God has given you. If you prefer a paper version, Peter Wagner's "Finding Your Spiritual Gifts" questionnaire is an easy-to-use self-assessment. There are several assessments online as well. http://www.efccl.org/gifts/ is an online Spiritual Gifts assessment. As you try things out, you will discover your abilities and so will mature leaders.

- **Confirmation**. Not only will leaders in the ministry confirm your gift, but through events and circumstances, God will also confirm your gift. As you use your gifts, you will see how much they bless others. As God confirms your gifts, you will also receive blessings.

Results of Activating Spiritual Gifts

There are several results for activating your Spiritual Gifts. Here are three of the most prominent results that make finding your gifts a worthwhile effort.

1. You will be **SATISFIED**.

    a. You will fulfill the destiny God has prepared for your life.

    b. You will become closer to God.

    c. You will make wiser decisions in every area of your life.

2. Others will be **EDIFIED**.

3. You will be an **EXAMPLE** to others as you exercise your gifts.

    a. You will encourage others to walk in their gifts.

    b. If you chose not to walk in your gift/s, you deprive the body of Christ of the gift of God in you. We are all part of the body of Christ. Other people need you and your gift.

    c. God will be **GLORIFIED**, which is your highest calling.

Stepping Stones

1. Spiritual gifts are supernatural abilities given through the Holy Spirit.

2. Spiritual gifts are given to encourage, strengthen, and increase the church.

3. Talents and spiritual gifts are two different things that sometimes work together.

4. Spiritual gifts must be activated in order to function.

5. The nine gifts listed in 1 Corinthians 12:1-11 are Word of Wisdom, Word of Knowledge, Discerning of Spirits, Gift of Faith, Gifts of Healing, Working of Miracles, Gift of Prophecy, Gift of Tongues, Interpretation of Tongues.

6. Motivational gifts include, but are not exclusive to the gift of helps, exhortation, administration, giving, mercy, and leadership.

7. The five ministry gifts in Ephesians 4:11-12 are apostle, prophet, evangelist pastor, and teacher.

8. A Christian can have gifts they never use. You are responsible for discovering, developing, and using your gifts.

9. Your gifts will glorify God, edify other people, and bring satisfaction to you.

10. Tools for walking in spiritual gifts are reading the Word, praying, training, and actively trying out your gifts.

I Am Supernatural

WALKING IN SPIRITUAL GIFTS

1. Define spiritual gifts. Explain their purpose.

2. How are spiritual gifts different from talents?

3. Name three conditions necessary to function in your spiritual gifts.

4. List the gift under the correct description: Faith, Word of Knowledge, Prophecy, Interpretation of Tongues, Word of Wisdom, Healing, Miracles, Discerning of spirits, and Diverse Tongues.

GIFTS of UTTERANCE	GIFTS of POWER	GIFTS of REVELATION

5. List at least five more gifts found in the body of Christ.

Glossary

SIMPLE GLOSSARY OF A FEW WORDS FROM THE CHRISTIAN FAITH

Adultery - The act of being sexually unfaithful to one's spouse

Agape - Affection, goodwill, love, brotherly love, a love feast

Angel - Messenger of God

Apostasy - Turning away from the religion, faith, or principles that one used to believe

Apostle - One sent forth, one chosen and sent with a special commission as a fully authorized representative of the sender.

Atonement - To cover, blot out, forgive; restore harmony between two individuals.

Attribute – An inherent characteristic

Backslide - To go back to ungodly ways of believing or acting.

Blasphemy - Words or actions showing a lack of respect for God or anything sacred.

Bless - To make or call holy, to ask God's favor, to praise; to make happy.

Blessing - A prayer asking God's favor for something, something that brings joy or comfort.

Born-again – To be begotten or birthed from God, the beginning, to start anew

Carnal - Of the flesh or body, not of the spirit, worldly; seat of one's desires opposed to the spirit of Christ

Cherubim - Guardian angels, angels that guard or protect places

Commitment - A promise, a pledge

Conditional - Placing restrictions, conditions, or provisions to receive

Conversion - Turn, return, turn back; change

Convert - To change from one form or use to another, to change from one belief or religion to another.

Courtship - The act or process of seeking the affection of one with the intent of seeking to win a pledge of marriage

Covenant - A pledge, alliance, agreement

Cult - A body of believers whose doctrine denies the deity of Christ.

Deliverance - A freeing or being freed, rescue; the act of change or transformation.

Demon - Evil spirit

Devil - Principal title for satan, the archenemy of God and man

Dispensation - A period of time, sometimes called ages

Dominion - To rule over, have power over, overcome, exercise lordship over

Eros - Erotic, physical love

Eternal - Existing always, forever, without time

Evangelist - Proclaims the gospel of Jesus Christ

Faith - Believing, trusting, depending, and relying on God

Fellowship - Sharing, communion, partnership, intimacy

Forgiveness - To pardon, release from bondage

Fornication - To act like a harlot, to be unfaithful to God, illicit sexual intercourse

Glorification - Salvation of the body, transforming mortal bodies to eternal bodies

Grace - Unmerited favor of God, help given in the time of need from a loving God

Holy - Set apart, sacred

Intercession - To meet or encounter, to strike upon, to pray for another

Justification - Salvation of the spirit, just as if I never sinned

Marriage - A divine institution designed by God as an intimate union, which is physical, emotional, intellectual, social, and most importantly, spiritual

New Testament - Text of the new covenant

Offering - Everything you give beyond your tithe

Old Testament - Text of the old covenant

Omnipotent - All-encompassing power of God

Omnipresent - Unlimited nature of God, ability to be everywhere at all times

Omniscient - God's power to know all things

Pastor - Shepherds of the body of believers

Philia - Conditional love, based on feelings, friendships

Praise - Thanksgiving, to say good things about, words that show approval.

Prayer - Communication with God

Prophet - One who is a spokesperson for God, one who has seen the message of God and declares that message

Propitiation - To satisfy the anger of God, to gain favor; appease

Rapture - To be carried away, or the catching away of

Reconciliation - Restore harmony or fellowship between individuals, to make friendly again

Redemption - To buy back, to purchase, recover, to Rescue from sin

Regeneration - To give new life or force to, renew, to be restored, to make better, improve or reform, to grow back anew

Repent - To give new life or force, to renew, to be restored, to make better, improve or reform, to grow back a new.

Resurrection - A return to life subsequent to death

Revelation - The act of revealing or making known

Righteousness - Right standing with God, integrity, virtue, purity of life, correctness of thinking

Sacrifice - The act of offering something, giving one thing for the sake of another; a loss of profit

Salvation - Deliverance from any kind of evil whether material or spiritual, being saved from danger or evil; to rescue.

Sanctification - Salvation of the soul. Separation from the seduction of sin

Satan - The chief of fallen spirits, opponent; adversary

Sealing - Something that guarantees, a sign or token, to make with a seal to make it official or genuine

Sin - All unrighteousness, missing the mark, wrong or fault; violation of the law

Spirit - A being that is not of this world, has no flesh or bones

Steward - A guardian or overseer of someone else's property, manager

Supernatural - Departing from what is usual, normal, or natural to give the appearance of transcending the laws of nature

Talent - A natural skill that is unusual.

Tithe - Ten percent of all your increase

Tribulation - Distress, trouble, a pressing together, pressure, affliction

Trinity - Three in one: Father, Son, Holy Spirit

Unconditional - No restrictions, conditions, boundaries, demands, or specific provisions

Will – Choice, inclination, desire, pleasure, command, what one wishes or determines shall be done

About the Author

Pamela is a teacher, mentor, and author of the inspirational book *Destiny Arise* and children's books including *Time in a Tuna*. Pam earned her bachelor's degree at the University of Illinois Springfield, her master's degree in Organizational Leadership at Lincoln Christian University, and her doctorate in Leadership at Christian Leadership University. She serves as a mentor for the Spirit Life Circles sponsored by CLU.

She works from her home in the prairie land of central Illinois. Pam and her bodybuilding husband own a gym/fitness center that promotes living a balanced life. She taught sixth grade for almost twenty years. Pam also taught preschool through adult-age students in various venues. She served as director of Super Church, the children's ministry in the United Methodist Church in her hometown. Pam also served in the church nursery, as director of New Life Ministries Discipleship Program, Vacation Bible School Director, Kingdom Kids Children's Ministry Director, and Sunday School teacher. She has also been on missionary trips. Her favorite trip, so far, was the time she spent in Belize.

Pam enjoys kayaking, bicycling, and riding her motor scooter. When she isn't writing, she enjoys spending time with her four children and their families which includes five grandchildren who are the inspiration of her children's books.

Walking with Jesus Series

BECOMING THE BEST ME I CAN BE

Book 1 - There Must Be a Better Way

Walking in Salvation

Book 2 - Lord, I Need Help!

Walking with the Holy Spirit

Book 3 - I Thought I Was Changed

Walking in Transformation

Book 4 - I Am Supernatural

Walking in Spiritual Gifts

Book 5 - I Am Strong

Walking as a Warrior

Book 6 - I Am Fruitful

Walking in the Fruit of the Spirit

Book 7 - Love Letters from God

Walking in the Word

Book 8 - Time in the Garden

Walking in the Power of Prayer

Book 9 - I'm in Charge of What?

Walking in Stewardship

Book 10 - The End of – Well, Pretty Much Everything

Walking into Eternity

Who am I? What am I doing here? Where am I going? Everyone at some point in life asks these questions. You were wired to ask and engineered to pursue the answers. The road to discovering destiny is besieged by fiascoes, failures, and the agony of defeat. If your strength has been depleted and has caused you to give up, sit down, push pause, and snooze until another day, then this book is just for you! Amazing experiences are waiting for you. Get ready to be awakened from the posture of defeat, depression, and despair.

Destiny Arise is an easy-to-read book, providing tools to aid in living an amazing life. This book is designed as a trip adviser for your expedition. It will teach you how to evict the spirit of mediocrity and use your past to propel you into your future. You will learn how to shake off the common, arising to be an uncommon force taking your rightful place in the earth. You can change the world. I pray this book will ignite a passionate fire to pursue your destiny unapologetically. Destiny, awake from your slumber and arise.

CPSIA information can be obtained
at www.ICGtesting.com
Printed in the USA
BVHW091209030122
625355BV00010B/447

9 781737 080268